MY OWN PICTURE DICTIONARY

Illustrated by
Peter Adby & Alan Fredman

AWARD PUBLICATIONS
London

ISBN 0-86163-880-8

First published 1984
This edition first published 1997
Second impression 2001

Published by Award Publications Limited,
27 Longford Street, London NW1 3DZ

Printed in Belgium

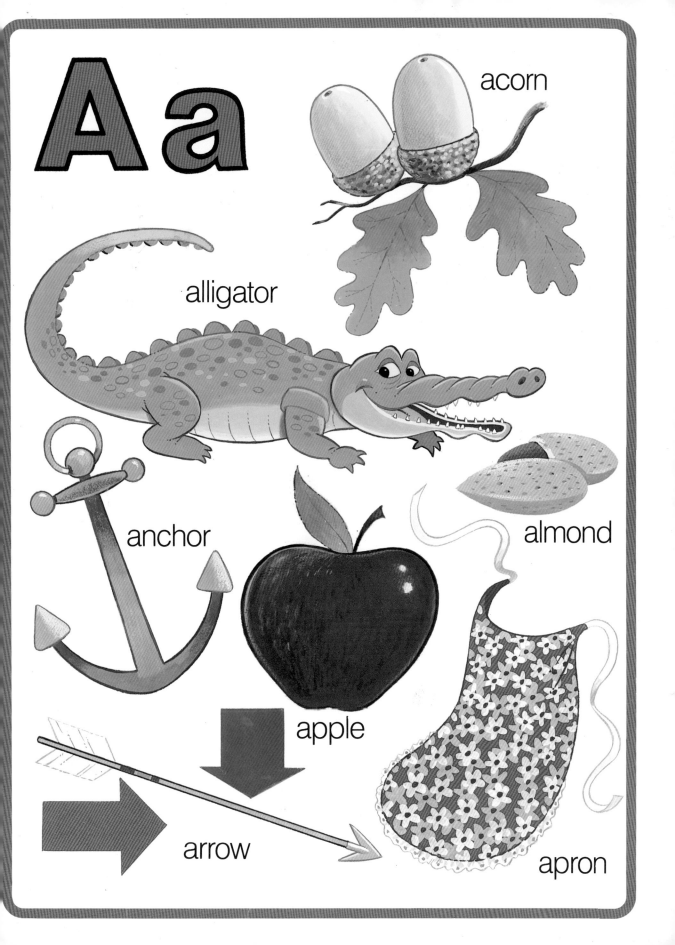

A a

acorn

alligator

anchor

almond

apple

arrow

apron

Bb

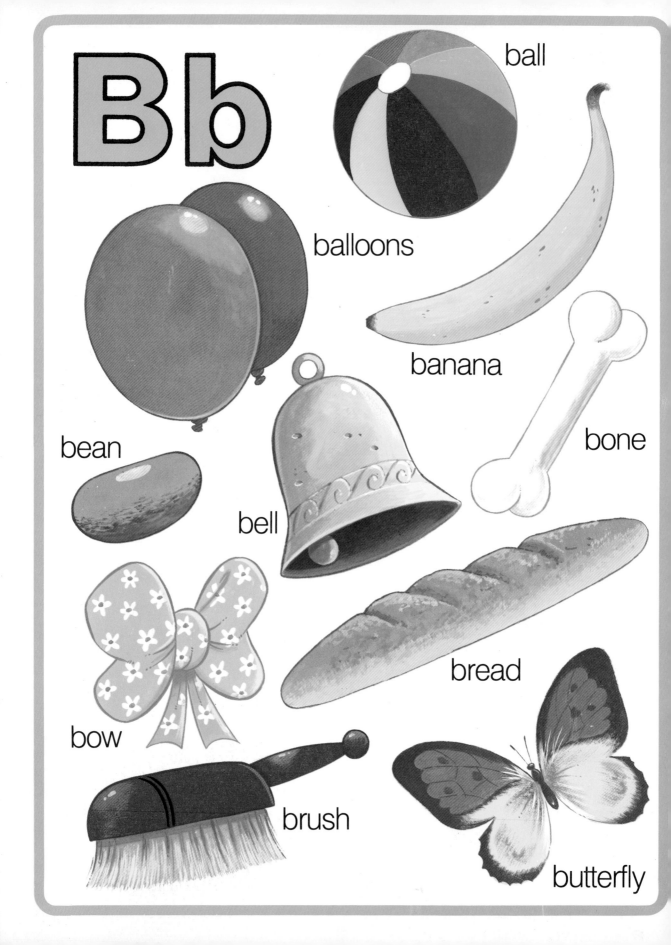

ball

balloons

banana

bean

bell

bone

bow

bread

brush

butterfly

Cc

candles

cake

carrot

cat

clock

clown

cup

cactus

cushion

Dd

dart

desk

dishes

drum

doll

duck

dog

Ee

earth

eagle

egg

ear

eggcup

8
eight

elephant

envelope

eskimo

F f

face

feather

fir

fish

feather

flowers

flute

frog

Gg

gate

glass

girl

gold

gong

gorilla

grapes

Hh

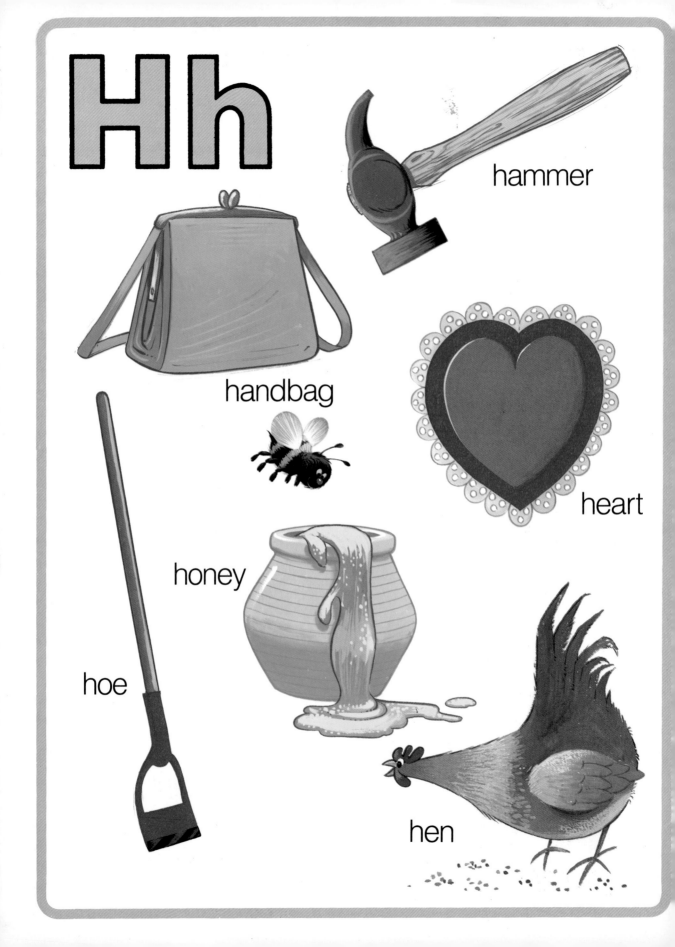

hammer

handbag

heart

honey

hoe

hen

Ii

icecream

igloo

indian

ivy

Jj

jewels

jug

jam

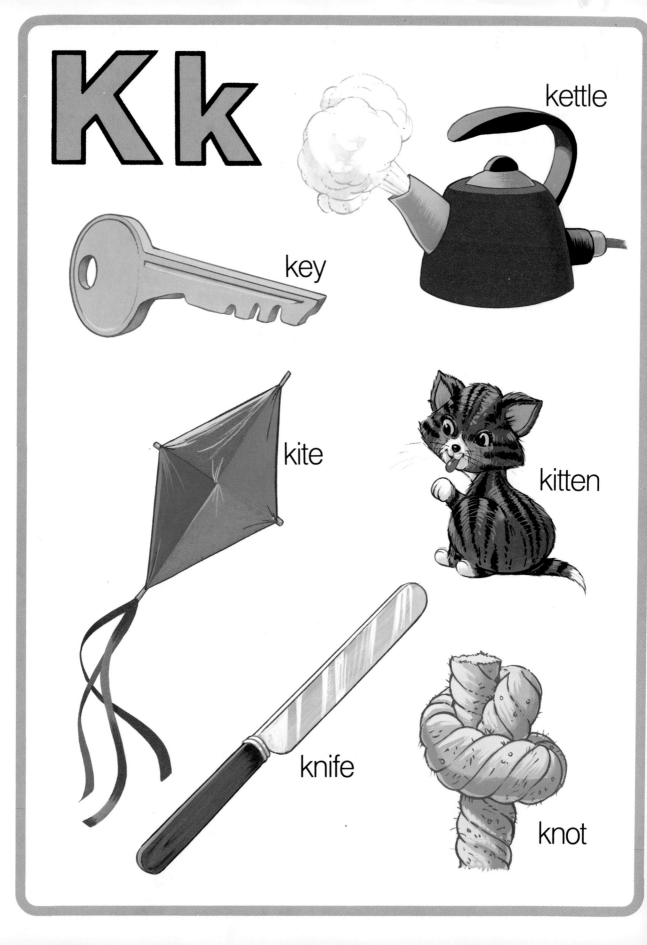

K k

kettle

key

kite

kitten

knife

knot

Ll

lamb

leaf

leek

log

lemon

ladder

lobster

lollipops

Mm

marrow

milk

mittens

mop

mouse

mushroom

monkey

mug

Nn

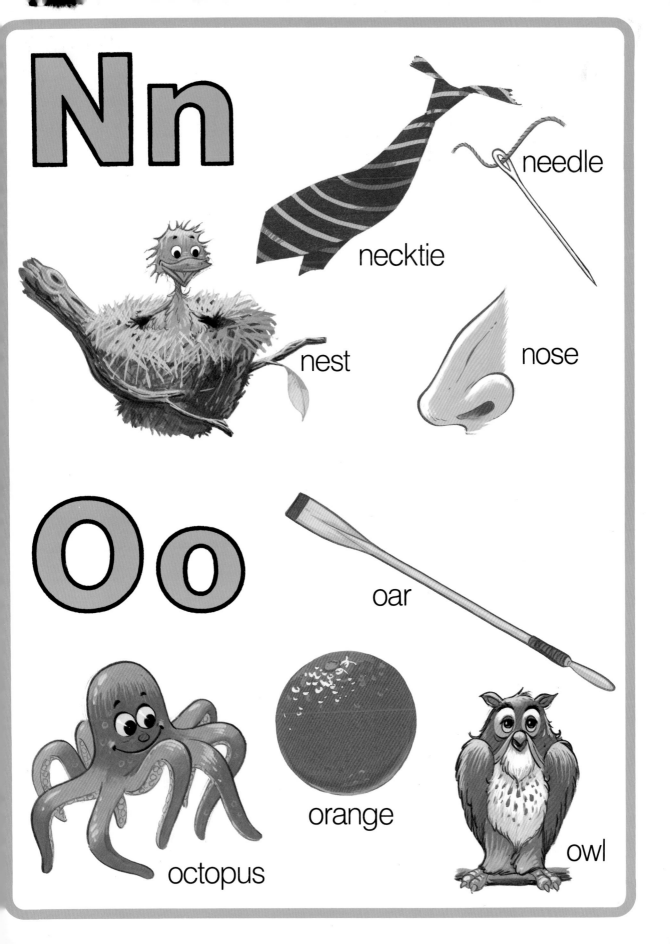

necktie

needle

nest

nose

Oo

oar

octopus

orange

owl

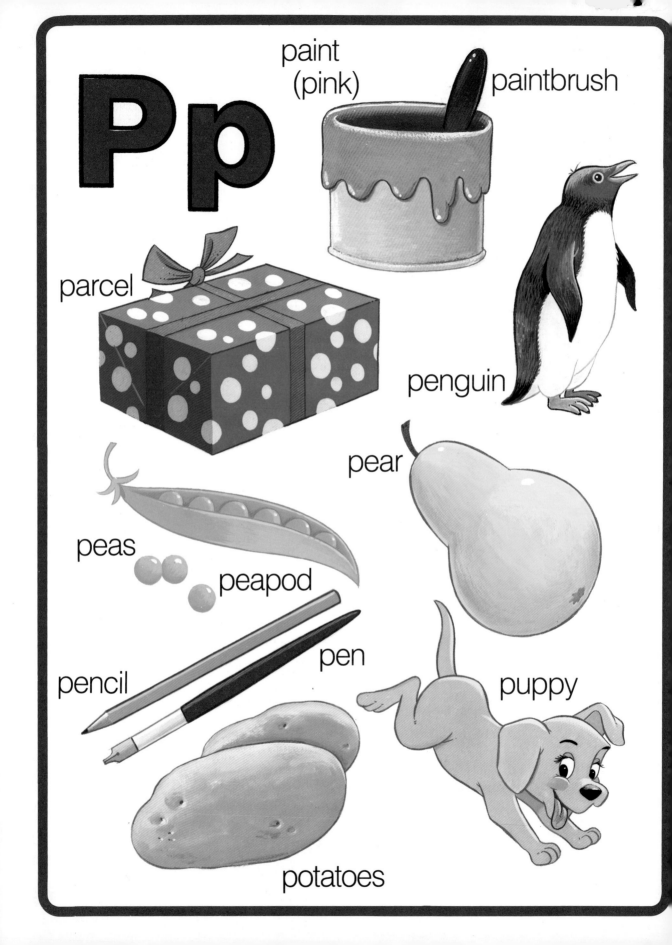

Pp

paint
(pink)

paintbrush

parcel

penguin

peas

peapod

pear

pencil

pen

puppy

potatoes

Qq

queen

quill

quilt

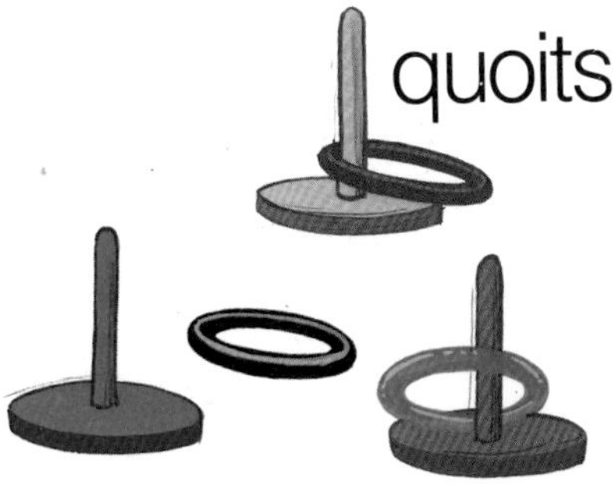

quoits

Rr

radishes

robin

rose

Ss

spoon

slippers

squirrel

swan

Tt

teapot

tomato

trumpet

tortoise

U u

umbrella

unicorn

uniform

V v

vulture

vase

violin

W w

watch

window

whale

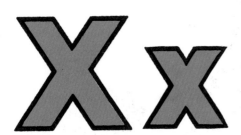

X x

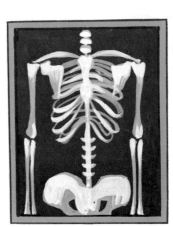

x-ray

xylophone